CW01506668

Forew

Though 1992 marks a notable milestone in the history of Lancashire League cricket – the League's centenary year, in fact – it has not been the intention that this book should be a history of that period.

Clearly the league, recognised throughout the cricketing world as the greatest of its kind over those one hundred years, has a history of encyclopaedic proportions which, it may be, others will attempt to chronicle.

The aim here has simply been to luxuriate nostalgically in some of the glories of the league's past, mainly the golden years of the thirties and the fifties, drawing largely on the author's personal memories and close friendships with many of the famous players who have helped to shape the sporting history of this small corner of Lancashire over the years, hopefully bringing some humour and some facts from behind the scenes as well as jogging other memories of deeds on the field of play itself.

If this book gives one hundredth of the pleasure to its readers that the Lancashire League in its golden years has given to the author then he will feel amply compensated for having put pen to paper.

THE GREATEST SHOW ON TURF

by
NOEL WILD

To commemorate the centenary
of
The Lancashire Cricket League

Hendon Publishing: Nelson

First published in Great Britain 1992
by Hendon Publishing Co. Ltd.,
Hendon Mill, Nelson, Lancashire.

ISBN 0 86067 146 1

Printed and bound by the Amadeus Press Ltd.,
Huddersfield, West Yorkshire HD2 1YJ

Contents

Most of the photographs in this book have been supplied with the compliments of the *Lancashire Evening Telegraph*

Chapter One

Constantine The Great

Measured seismically on the Richter Scale of international cricket there was this earthquake.

Its name was Learie Nicholas Constantine. And when anybody dips into the cornucopian treasure chest of Lancashire League memories over its one hundred years of sunshine history it is the solitaire diamond which sparkles most of all.

Learie Constantine, grandson of a West Indian slave, was the first black man that the mill folk of Nelson, Lancashire, had ever seen when he arrived between the satanic factory chimneys in the clogs-and-shawl days of 1929. He was, in his own words, 'a coloured curiosity'. Youngsters would peep through his front room window to get a glimpse of 'the man with the black face'.

One asked quite innocently as he walked down Leeds Road on his first day in the town: 'Has ta' bin down t' coal 'ole, mister?'

Learie had to have that translated!

He told me: 'I nearly funked and went back home.'

Fortunately his wife Norma counselled him wisely: 'Give them a chance to get used to us,' she told him. 'They may grow to accept us, even to like us.'

As it turned out Nelson folk grew to love them.

He stayed in the town for twenty years, was made a Freeman of the Borough, and later, of course, was first knighted and then elevated to the House of Lords as 'Baron Constantine of Maraval in Trinidad and of Nelson in the County Palatine of Lancaster'.

It was as a cricketer, however, that he is remembered most. An explosive volcanic cricketer the likes of which the league had not seen before, has not seen since and in all probability will never see again.

There have been better batsmen in the league, better fast bowlers, but never, never a better fieldsman. Learie had something extra, however: ebullience, effervescence, fizz, call it what you will. It was certainly showmanship aligned to brilliant all-round athleticism and skills which brought the Lancashire League crowds to their feet in awe, admiration and sometimes hostility for nine glorious seasons with Nelson Cricket Club; nine seasons during which the Nelson club won the league championship no fewer than seven times.

When he bowled he was both fast and ferocious. When he batted he was titanic, always geared to strike a monumental six rather than take a single. And in the field he was like a puma in any position.

He would take a catch at gully, even when the ball had been struck hard off the meat of the bat, and with speed, sleight of hand and flamboyance pocket the ball and then turn towards the boundary as though he had missed it.

Once, Ernest Bradshaw, one of his amateur colleagues, told me he leapt down the wicket to take a catch off his bowling right in front of Ernest who was fielding at forward short-leg. The crowds loved it.

The press dubbed him 'Old Electric Heels'.

The Lancashire League clubs – all of them, not only Nelson – reaped the harvest at the turnstiles. To such an extent, indeed, that once when Learie was on the point of leaving the Nelson club for league pastures elsewhere it is said that some other clubs got together to contribute towards his fee.

Of course it was not all Paradise. It was sometimes Rage in Heaven.

There was one particular match between Nelson and Colne, deadly 'Derby' rivals at the time, when, as Learie himself put it: 'It was not cricket; it was more like a bloody war.'

It was after this match that representatives of the two clubs plus Learie and Colne's professional at the time, Derbyshire's Archie Slater, were required to attend a specially convened Peace Conference at the Colne president's home.

Learie told me: 'I'd like to put this Nelson-Colne war into

perspective for the record. I had no Derby day hatred for Colne. I wanted to win – as always, but as a West Indian I did not feel the chronic, long-standing historical rivalry which existed between the two towns to a point where it was almost enmity.

'Amar Singh, who played for both Colne and Burnley, was a dear friend of mine, for instance – and a very great cricketer. I liked some of the amateur players, too – Leslie Bulcock for one. Tiny as he was he faced me unflinchingly at my fastest and has never complained to this day that I was unfair. But then, you see, he was a good cricketer as well as being a decent fellow.

'On the particular day in question, however, one or two of the Colne side deliberately set out to provoke me. They fired insults which were meant to wound and I have to say there was also some ill feeling between Slater and myself dating back to when the West Indians had played Derbyshire.

'Whenever Slater hit me on the pad, even if my leg was a yard down the wicket and six inches outside the leg stump, the whole field would appeal like a well-trained male voice choir. Once when they appealed a bit too early – just as I swept the ball very late to the boundary – I could not help but come to the conclusion that the whole thing was a pre-arranged affair to cheat me out.

'I was so angry that I must admit that when it came Colne's turn to bat I bowled hard and fast at the batsmen's ribs, kept the ball short on every batsman's body – and most of them got hits!

'They called this Peace Conference after the match. They asked Slater to behave himself and they asked me to withdraw my bumper barrage. After that the Nelson-Colne Derby games lost a lot of their cut-throat appeal. The next game, in fact, lost all its character – it was so tame it wasn't worth playing.

'How could they ask me to play Little Lord Fauntleroy!'

There was another occasion when Learie admitted to me that he bowled to hurt rather than to get a wicket.

It was when East Lancashire, the Blackburn club, visited Nelson with Jim Blanckenberg as their professional.

Blanckenberg, of course, was a South African and had been Nelson's professional immediately before Learie.

On this particular day, with the sun blazing down, Nelson's

Seedhill ground was a cauldron of emotional expectations. One of the biggest crowds ever to gather there, over ten thousand, awaited the confrontation of Nelson's past and present professionals.

Learie told me: 'I had met Blanckenberg just once previously when he stopped me in Carr Road, Nelson, and assured me that he held no animosity as regards my colour.

'When he came out to bat I walked up to his end to show Nelson people that there was no enmity so far as I was concerned and stretched out my hand to him in a gesture of friendship.

'Blanckenberg turned his back on me and walked away!

'I was furious. Hurt, insulted, but above all furious. And that day I bowled 'Bodyline' before the term had been invented.

'I don't mind telling you that I bowled like Hell let loose right at his body. I gave him a terrible beating and at the end of it he walked into our dressing room, naked except for a raincoat, and said to our skipper: "Look what that bloody pro. of yours has done to me." I am a black man, but that day I tell you Jimmy Blanckenberg was both black and blue.

'I will say this for him though – I have never seen a batsman stand up to the short ball and take blows to the body with so much courage. He never flinched as the ball thudded into him, never gave a sign of pain. He had tremendous guts – there is no doubt about that.'

Blanckenberg scored 77 runs that day before eventually being clean bowled – by Constantine.

'Of course, I was young in those days,' Learie explained to me.

'Today such insults would roll off my back like water. I don't think about black men or white men or yellow men; only about good men, indifferent men and bad men. Looking back on my cricketing days in the league I know that for every one insult there were ten thousand human expressions of warmth and friendship towards me.'

It was Learie's good fortune that his sense of humour was in tune with Lancashire's sense of humour.

'I am always prepared to laugh at myself,' he would say. 'I like laughing. We are not put on earth to cry if we can help it, are we?'

Though I was only a schoolboy when Learie was scorching the Lancashire League earth in the league's golden thirties we became great friends after the war.

We laughed and joked together in all sorts of hostelries – in the Station Hotel, Nelson, the Café Royal in London, the Wig and Pen Club in Fleet Street, the Red Lion pub in Earby, and, of course, at Nelson's ground – Seedhill.

Always, even when he became ill, there was the bubble of effervescence which had made him a legend and an idol among the cobbles and the mill chimneys of the town he was proud to call his second home.

'I got on this bus,' he would say. 'The conductor asked me one shilling and threepence for the fare. I knew it should only be a shilling and I told him so. "No," replied the conductor, "You're wrong. It's one shilling and threepence." So I turned to the white lady sitting next to me and asked: "Do you know the fare?" She said "Yes, you are quite right – it is one shilling." So I smiled at the conductor and said "Now do you believe me – now that you have got it in black and white." The conductor had a good laugh too.'

I had coffee with Learie and Norma at their last English home in Shoot Up Hill, close to Lord's Cricket Ground, where, in his prime, the vast crowd had risen to give him a standing ovation twice in one day. He was clearly never going to take the new ball at the pavilion end again. The infectious chuckle was still there. The spirit was still willing. But the body was weak.

The man we had called 'Electric Heels' had lost his voltage.

'Don't bother to get up,' I said as I bade my farewell.

And, as he often did when he met anyone from the Nelson area, he deliberately lapsed into a somewhat exaggerated northern dialect. 'Tha's bin a good pal, lad,' he said. 'Si thi soon.'

It was not to be.

Two weeks later, sadly, the King of them all was dead.

Wherever men talk about Lancashire League cricket, however, the dazzling all-round deeds of the man who came to us from a slave background and ended up in the House of Lords will remain indelible.

Chapter Two

The Fast Lane

Constantine was the signing which awakened other clubs in the league to the fact that the public wanted to see not just effective professionals but international stars. He was not, however, the first 'sensation' signing.

The first, again with Nelson setting the pace, was E. A. McDonald, of Victoria, Australia and later Lancashire.

Ted McDonald, in tandem with Gregory, had been the fast bowling force which shattered England's best in the 1921 Ashes tour and when Nelson announced that they had signed him for the following summer it was a coup which was to register shock waves in Australia – and in Yorkshire!

Australia's cricket authorities were positively alarmed at the prospect of losing, by some accounts, the finest fast bowler the game has ever seen.

Yorkshire's concern was the suggestion, later to become fact, that McDonald would use Nelson as a residential springboard from which he would qualify for Lancashire.

The Australian pressures on McDonald to renege on his promise to the Nelson club were enormous and during our winter of 1921-22 there were suggestions that he might do just that.

Lord Hawke, the autocratic uncrowned king of Yorkshire County Cricket Club at that time, went on record as being 'delighted to note McDonald's sound refusal' to join Nelson.

This led to a sharp exchange of words in a new, verbal War of the Roses. Mr Tom Morgan, the chairman of Nelson Cricket Club and normally a mild man, was considerably angered by

Hawke's interference and was moved to say at a public meeting: 'I am afraid Lord Hawke is only imperfectly informed of the position. McDonald has signed an agreement to play for Nelson for the next three years. This agreement has been in the hands of the secretary of the Lancashire League since August. There has been no attempt, either on one side or the other, to vary its conditions or to cancel it. McDonald has dealt with us honourably and straightforwardly and we are confident that he will fulfil his contract.'

McDonald duly did. And he graced the League, and later the county, with several years of fast bowling at its highest art form.

I did not see McDonald in action, but those who did, and some who played against him, have testified that he was something very special.

Was he, indeed, the best fast bowler ever to play in the league?

It is, of course, hypothetical, but if we are to play games with our heroes there is no doubt that there are many magnificent contenders for the crown in the fast lane.

E. A. 'Manny' Martindale, of Burnley, Lowerhouse and later Bacup, is just one of half a dozen West Indian speed kings for a start.

West Indians Charlie Griffith, Chester Watson, Roy Gilchrist, Wesley Hall, Michael Holding and Andy Roberts are others with clear claims.

From India we have Amar Singh, Dattu Phadkar and Kapil Dev.

From Pakistan Khan Mohammed and Fazal Mahmood.

From South Africa Eddie Barlow and Dik Abed.

From England Frank Tyson, and of course the great Sidney Barnes, regarded by many, including Constantine, as by far the greatest bowler ever to grace the game at any level.

From Australia Dennis Lillee, Neil Hawke, Geoff Lawson, and Ray Lindwall.

What a galaxy of fast shooting stars!

Purely on statistics Charlie Griffith clearly takes pride of place. He came to England, almost unknown outside Barbados, in 1963 with the West Indian touring party and by August that year had established himself as the most destructive fast bowler in the world at that time.

There have been fast bowlers hunting in pairs who have claimed dual fame throughout Test cricket history – Gregory and McDonald, Lindwall and Miller, Lillee and Thomson for Australia, Larwood and Voce, Trueman and Statham for England, Constantine and Martindale for the West Indies.

Griffith and Hall joined that exclusive band in 1963. And when Burnley duly signed the former in 1964 it proved to be one of the best moves the club ever made.

The club won the league championship, and was runner-up in the Worsley Cup knock-out competition before a crowd which paid then record receipts, and Griffith produced an all-time record of aggregate league victims – 144 wickets at an average of only 5.20 runs each.

It is a record which will not easily be beaten, if at all. And if, for that alone, anybody wants to argue that he was not the best fast bowler of all time in the league then it is going to have to be a powerful argument.

After that first league season there was controversy at Test level about the legitimacy of his fastest delivery. The late Ken Barrington startled most by affirming that Griffith was 'a chucker' and that he would therefore never bat against him again.

It was a major indictment against an international class bowler and one which was difficult either to sustain or disprove. All I can say is that Griffith came to Burnley with an unblemished record, and nobody – umpires, players or spectators – questioned his bowling action as he blasted his way to the league record.

I asked his erudite captain Derek Riley: 'Did Charlie really throw?'

And Riley replied: 'I honestly couldn't say. What I will say is that he threw them all or none at all.'

If that was the case then Charlie had been throwing or not throwing for several seasons before Barrington showed him the red card.

Charlie, himself, one of *Wisden's* Five Cricketers of the Year in 1963, told me only recently: 'I think that psychologically the accusations did me harm. You see for season after season, both in the West Indies and here in England, I had bowled without anybody even slightly suggesting I was a thrower. Then came this bombshell attack on my action. I think some batsmen may have been looking for a scapegoat for their own deficiencies.'

Statistically, as I say, the claim of Charlie Griffith's supporters for the Lancashire League's fast bowling crown is impossible to deny.

His fellow West Indian Roy Gilchrist's claim would also be difficult to fault. 'Gilly' – bouncer, beamer, deadly bowler for Bacup and Lowerhouse – had more ten wicket hauls than any other bowler I know. He was probably the fastest and easily the most ferocious of the league's post-war speed merchants.

If it comes to one single expression of physical supremacy on the cricket field then for me it has to be the first time I saw Gilchrist bowl. It occurred at Rochdale cricket ground where I had gone with Rochdale's professional of the day, Dattu Phadkar, India's superb all-rounder, who, of course, also played for Nelson and Burnley. Gilchrist was playing with Middleton at the time and Middleton took the field first.

The wicket was greasy on top, hard underneath. You did not have to be an expert on pitch conditions to know that the ball would react capriciously and certainly fly around the ears quite a bit.

Gilchrist certainly knew.

And George Holland, who was to open innings for Rochdale, knew.

I was told afterwards that the Rochdale team stood back, as gentlemen would, to give George first use of the toilet half an hour before the game started!

George and I were friendly acquaintances, but he did not say all that much as he passed me on the way to the wicket that day.

He said even less on his way back!

A slightly-built man, George took guard as Gilchrist paced about impatiently and snorted ominously some forty yards away. This, by the way, was in the days when the mere thought of a batsman wearing headgear would have been considered effeminate. Gilchrist's first ball was a bouncer, yards over George Holland's head, practically knocking the sightscreen over at one bounce.

The next ball had the effect of a Mills bomb! A bouncer again, but this time only just short of a length, it lifted sharply at terrifying speed, knocked George's middle molar out of its socket, dislodged off-and leg-side fangs, dumped George on his behind in a pool of blood, and ricocheted to break the wicket.

The score-book, I imagine, would record: 'G. Holland, poleaxed, bemused, retired hurt requiring extensive dental repair, and clean bowled Gilchrist, 0.'

It would not be an overstatement to say that the reaction in the Rochdale dressing room was less than wildly ecstatic. They carted George off to the nearest orthodontist. And sent out a search party for the next man in!

No doubt about it – Griffith and Gilchrist were two very mean, moody and magnificent speed merchants.

However, if pressed as to which Lancashire League fast bowler I would choose to open the bowling for an all-time World XI, I would have to go for Australia's Lindwall.

As I say I did not see McDonald and therefore cannot consider him, but Lindwall I did see in action often and when he ran in to bowl it was with a balance and grace I had not seen before. With rhythm in every stride of his run-up, he gently accelerated until he reached the bowling crease like a coiled spring to deliver a lightning missile aimed unerringly at a trembling off stump and leaving the batsman no alternative but to prod myopically forward as the ball veered into the slips.

I have to admit that in his early days for Nelson he was not all that successful. He was bowling Test match lengths and Test match out-swingers to league batsmen and league slip fielders. However, he was quick to learn that in league cricket you have to bowl at the stumps. He therefore accordingly developed an in-swinger and introduced more frequently his high-speed yorker right into the block hole. The result was that after taking only 33 wickets in the first half of the 1952 season he took 63 in the second.

The figures do not come near to matching some of the other pacemen who have scorched the league turf, but he was a thoroughbred fast bowler and, for me, the best.

Chapter Three

Bradman

The brightest asteroid of all in the galaxy of Lancashire League megastars over the century is undoubtedly the one that twinkled but then, at the very last minute, faded – Sir Donald Bradman.

Bradman, incomparably the greatest batsman the game has ever produced, came within a whisker of signing as professional for Accrington in 1931.

The Accrington club offered Bradman terms after the legendary Australian had emaciated England's bowlers at Leeds to amass a then record Test score for a single innings of 334 in 1930.

It was by far the most audacious league cricket bid of all time.

Bradman himself has written: 'I was contemplating my own future when Learie Constantine enquired whether I would be interested in playing cricket in the Lancashire League.'

The first tentative approach to the great man was made in the form of a radiogram to a person apparently acting on Bradman's behalf, one Claude Spencer.

It was from 'Nelson, Lancs.' And it was signed 'Constantine.' No particular club was mentioned.

More cables signed 'Bradman' and 'Constantine' followed, and when the Australian press got wind of what was afoot the headlines screamed in agony.

'Shall we lose Bradman?' they asked.

'The discussions are so secret,' one Australian newspaper reported, 'that even Bradman is not aware of the name of the club involved.'

Accrington, however, turned out to be that club, and a later newspaper report stated: 'The Lancashire County club is interested in the Accrington proposal. Bradman is reported to be considering two seasons as qualification period in the league and then joining the county, which is probably backing Accrington financially.'

Shades of McDonald, Nelson, and the Old Trafford hierarchy!

Eventually there was a radiogrammed firm offer from Accrington. It read:

> Terms from Accrington to Bradman, Sydney. Confirming telephone conversation. Arrive England April 18. Duties finish September 3. Play 30 matches, 20 of these on Saturdays. Duration match, five hours. Attend evenings. No groundwork. We offer fee £600. Estimate £150 talent money and collections. Every confidence £150 exhibition matches. Contract two years. We pay passage both ways. Board residence costs you £2 weekly. We understand *Sunday Chronicle* offer you £150 for cricket articles. Prospect of other business arrangements. Decision expected and desired in seven days if possible. Conditions similar to Constantine.
>
> It was signed 'Holgate'.

The late Mr Gideon Holgate was at that time secretary of the Accrington club.

The terms may seem somewhat derisory by today's standards, but with the average working man's wage around thirty shillings (£1.50p) a week in the early 1930s the Accrington offer to the world's greatest batsman was really most handsome.

However, Australian big business interests were by now beginning to swing into action. There was a tremendous round-robin of business cash generated to persuade Bradman to stay in his homeland, and on 30th October 1931, Gideon Holgate received this cablegram:

'To Holgate, Accrington CC. Regret decline your offer. Appreciate pleasant nature of negotiations. Writing full details – Bradman.'

Thus the world's most destructive batsman ever evaded the

league at the eleventh hour.

Had it been otherwise there is little doubt that the man with a Test batting average of 99.9 would have surpassed all the other great batsmen who have graced our league grounds.

In Bradman's absence we are left to ponder on the relative brilliance of some of the others.

There have been so many radiantly shining stars over the years.

Australian Alan Fairfax, who came to Accrington instead of Bradman, another magnificent Australian, Bobby Simpson, and South African Eddie Barlow with the same club.

Sydney Barnes and Wally Langdon of Australia, Collie Smith of West Indies, and Mudassar Nazar of Pakistan – all with Burnley.

Polly Umrigar of India at Church.

Bill Alley and Ray Flockton of Australia, Stanley Jayasinghe of Sri Lanka, and Collis King of West Indies at Colne.

Peter Philpott, Alan Border and Tom Moody of Australia at East Lancashire.

Clyde Walcott and Conrad Hunte of West Indies at Enfield.

George Headley and Clive Lloyd of West Indies, and Vinoo Mankad of India at Haslingden.

Roy Marshall and Basil Butcher of West Indies at Lowerhouse.

Saeed Ahmed of Pakistan, Graham Roope of England, Larry Gomes of West Indies, and Steve Waugh and more recently Joe Scuderi of Australia at Nelson.

Gul Mohammed of India, Seymour Nurse of West Indies, and Ian Chappell of Australia at Ramsbottom.

Vijay Hazare of India at Rawtenstall.

Viv Richards of West Indies, and Peter Sleep of Australia at Rishton.

Jim Burke and Neil Dansie of Australia at Todmorden.

All these and many more have decorated our league summers with grace and power and personality.

Colne's Alley was both elegant and arrogant at the crease. I have not seen any player 'farm' the bowling so well, nor a player who could dictate the opposing captain's field placings so ruthlessly.

Haslingden's Headley, of course, was the first batsman to

introduce technique to the West Indian game; a brilliant executioner of bowlers fast or slow even measured by the highest standards.

Clive Lloyd who served the same club is another who could dominate any game at any level: league, Test or county, with an array of strokes rarely equalled.

Accrington's Bob Simpson produced a flow of runs which was almost impossible to stem when he was in full flight.

And Viv Richards, though having only one rain-affected season with Rishton, was, of course, almost a law unto himself as he sprayed the boundaries like a machine gun.

They were all world class. Even so one other outshone them all.

That was Everton Weekes who thundered and plundered at Bacup for seven glorious seasons in the fifties. As a league batsman he was in a class of his own. When he was on song you simply could not bowl to him. He would lean, almost lazily, on the back foot and hit you square past point with a power that was awesome. Or smash you through mid-wicket with a velocity beyond normal men. Or cover drive magnificently.

You could not bowl to him with any sort of tactical plan simply because he defied all tactics and destroyed all plans. He could pick up the fastest of the pace bowlers as the ball left their hands, and as regards the sleight-of-hand spinners he did not need to scrutinise their actions – he could actually see which way the ball was spinning whilst it was in flight.

Weekes scored over one thousand runs in each of his seven seasons with Bacup, defying both the elements and some of the very best international fast and spin bowling of his day. He scored the league's record 'time limit' aggregate of 1,518 runs in 1951, and ended the 1954 season with an incredible average of 158.25 runs per completed innings! Neither Bobby Simpson, who scored 1,444 runs for Accrington in 1959, nor Viv Richards were quite a match for that.

Weekes, of course, was also the total destroyer in the Test cricket of his day, forming alongside Clyde Walcott and Sir Frank Worrell the famous 'Three W's' who tore England's bowling apart in the fifties.

He still keeps in touch with Bacup, but now, at 66 years of age, has chosen a less physically active game. He has represented West Indies – at bridge! It was a card game he began playing in his Bacup days, and if he handles the cards half as well as he handled the cricket bat then it will be grand slams all the way.

Chapter Four

In a Spin

I am in a bit of a spin – about the league's spinners.

Who *was* the best?

There have been so many, and so many different types, different styles, different deceits. And all world class.

Bruce Dooland and Colin McCool were two right-arm leg-spinners of the highest Australian Test ranking who played for East Lancashire between 1949 and 1954.

There was the diminutive Indian sorcerer S. P. 'Fergie' Gupte who spun the ball like an angry wasp to take 136 wickets for Rishton at just over nine runs each in 1955.

Jim McConnon of England, Lance Gibbs of West Indies and Cecil George Pepper of Australia – all spun for Burnley.

There was Jack Manning and Johnny Martin at Colne, Vinoo Mankad at Haslingden, Johnny Wardle at Nelson and Rishton, George Tribe at Rawtenstall, Tony Lock at Ramsbottom, Brian Close at Todmorden, and going back quite a bit, even one Hedley Verity at Accrington.

The best?

It would clearly depend to a considerable extent on what type of wicket we might be talking about.

The wrist spinners – Dooland, McCool, Pepper, Gupte, Wardle and Tribe – would turn the ball either way on almost any pitch though sometimes sacrificing accuracy.

The orthodox finger spinners, left arm or right – Manning, McConnon, Lock, Mankad and company – were always more accurate and often more effective when there was some undeniable 'turn' in the pitch itself.

Yorkshire's Wardle, of course, conjured up every trick in the left-armer's book – either orthodox leg-breaks or wrist spin which turned either way or went straight through, plus flight and pace variation – it really was a baffling mix.

His figures during his four seasons with Nelson and six with Rishton reveal that he averaged nearly 100 wickets a season – in total 950 to be precise – and at a cost of only 11 runs each. He took more wickets than any other bowler in the league on three occasions, and in one season, 1964, he produced his best figures – 122 wickets. Wardle's is certainly a most impressive record over a long period.

Of Lock and McConnon it can be argued that, brilliant and proved as they were in the Test arena, they did not stay around long enough in the league to come fully into the reckoning.

Mankad, of course, is difficult to ignore. He stepped right out of the league, with Haslingden's permission, to perform magnificently for India against England in 1952, and was clearly a left-arm spin bowler of the very highest class.

Dooland, too, is hard to pass by. He played for Bradman's post-war Australians at a time when 'Down Under' cricket was absolutely bristling with front-line bowlers of every denomination. McCool likewise, though personally I could not rate him in Dooland's class.

As I say, it is a teaser of enormous proportions to be asked who was the best of all. At the end of the day, however, I have to come down in preference for the man who did not play Test cricket at all, save in the unofficial 1945 'Victory' Tests.

The name is C. G. Pepper.

Pepper really was a batsman's living death. He bowled – leg-breaks, right arm, googlies, top spinners, flippers, 'quick, quick, slow'. And he bowled with the determination of a man who expected a wicket with every ball.

He was also, of course, a titanic batsman. And an incredible character.

Having lunch with Pepper is hot stuff.

'Ian Botham!' he will snort. 'Botham! The best all-rounder since the war? Hell, he wouldn't have got into the New South Wales dressing room in my day. Good God, I could have bowled him out with a cabbage – even with the outside leaves still on! And as a bowler . . . well, frankly, even if somebody had paid to get him into our New South Wales team I doubt if Bradman would have put him on to bowl. Hell, we had Lindwall hadn't we? And Keith Miller. And me!'

Bradman, himself, once rated Pepper the second-best right-arm leg-spin/googly bowler ever – second only to the incomparable Bill 'Tiger' O'Reilly.

I have mentioned the great England and Yorkshire left-arm spinner, Hedley Verity. It is not widely known that he was professional for Accrington in 1927 – and a failure.

Verity, who was killed leading his men into action in Italy in 1943, had an almost apologetic shuffle to the wicket and the most innocent and economic of arm actions, but he was a great spin bowler measured by any era. On a sticky wicket he was unplayable and even on a perfect batting strip, he was difficult. The Australians, including Bradman, found him the most skilful spin bowler of his day, and yet his one season at Accrington yielded only 67 wickets. The truth of the matter, of course, was that the Verity who played for Accrington was then only beginning to master his trade. His best was yet to come.

The same cannot be said, however, of Hugh Tayfield, the South African off-spinner who played for East Lancashire in 1956. Tayfield was already a Test bowler rated by many as the best of his kind in the world, but neither his reputation nor his spin cut any ice with the league's batsmen. They hammered him unmercifully.

On the whole, however, the spinners, and particularly the wrist spin specialists, have had great success over the sunshine years and, like the fast bowlers, they learned quickly that the key to success was to bowl at the stumps.

Pepper, who would bowl the googly only sparingly as a surprise ball in first-class cricket, took more league wickets with that delivery from the back of the hand and with his top-spinner than with his leg-breaks.

There is little doubt that had he not fallen foul of the Australian cricket authorities in 1946 he would have galvanised the Test scene throughout the forties and fifties. Purely as a spin sorcerer, not to mention his batting, he was vastly superior to the other Australian spinners of the day, people like McCool, Douglas Ring, and even Dooland.

'I always got on well with Bradman,' he will tell you. 'Still do. But I got the little sod out twice in one innings and the umpire wouldn't give him out. When I told the umpire what I thought of his decisions I was expected to apologise. I wouldn't. And I came to England.'

Nelson could have signed him in the summer of 1946 but for once failed to appreciate that they had one of the world's best players within their grasp. And Rochdale reaped the benefit of his brilliance for three seasons in which he performed the 1,000 runs, 100 wickets 'double' three times in successive seasons in the Central Lancashire League.

When he joined Burnley in 1949 the pundits said he would never do the 'double' in the Lancashire League. Nobody ever had, not even Constantine. But Pepper did – in his first season!

Chapter Five

The All-Rounders

I have referred to Learie Constantine and to Cecil George Pepper as the great all-rounders of the League's two golden eras – the thirties and the fifties.

There were, of course, many other West Indians and Australians to challenge for their crowns.

From the West Indies we have had Weekes, the master batsman, who learned to bowl off-spin to no little effect, and Walcott who, in addition to his powerful batting could cause a few stumps to tremble at his medium pace.

We also had, for all too short a spell, chunky Collie Smith, who, had he not been killed in a car crash, would surely have developed into one of Test cricket's all-time greats.

Collie, professional for Burnley in 1958 and 1959, scored 309 runs for Burnley against Lowerhouse in his second season to create a new record for the League's Worsley Cup competition, the previous best having been Weekes' 225 for Bacup against Rawtenstall a year earlier. He was a magnificent right-hand batsman, probably second only to Sir Gary Sobers in the West Indies at that time. He was also developing nicely as an off-spin bowler.

From Australia, too, there were several who, though specialists with either the bat or the ball, were also richly prominent in the all-rounder category – Bruce Dooland, George Tribe, Jack Pettiford, Neil Hawke, Bill Alley, and, more recently, Colin Miller.

However, when it comes to all-rounders in the full sense of the word the brightest jewels in the Lancashire League's crown, after

Constantine, commoner and peer of the Realm. Above, the grandson of a slave, playing dominoes in the tap room of the Red Lion pub, Earby, with Colne's Les Bulcock and West Indian Alf Charles (fourth and fifth from the left) looking on, and below, as 'Baron Constantine' with the Duke of Norfolk, former President of the M.C.C.

O. G. 'Collie' Smith, West Indies and Burnley, who would surely have rivalled the legendary Sir Garfield Sobers had he not been killed in a car crash. One of only five batsmen in the League's 100-year history to hit a straight six into the football field and still holder of the League's Worsley Cup record score.

Ray Lindwall, Australia and Nelson – the purest fast bowler of them all?

Eddie Paynter, Enfield's tiny giant of the league's amateurs. The man who left his sick bed to win the Ashes for England on the tour of Australia of 1932-33.

Yet another of the 'Three W's' – Clyde Walcott, West Indies and Enfield.

Cecil George Pepper, New South Wales and Burnley – in the author's view the best spin bowler the League has seen and one of the great all-rounders.

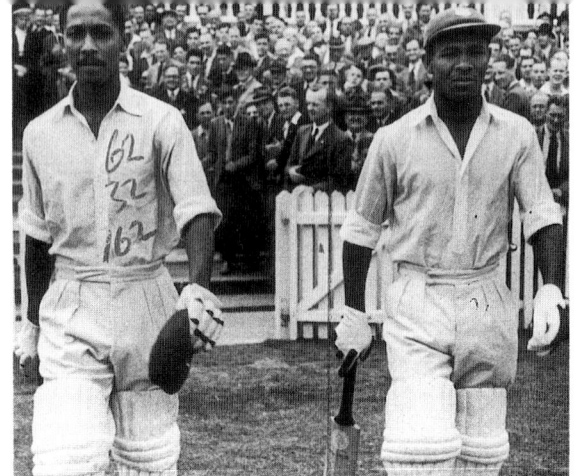

On the right, Everton de Courcy Weekes, almost certainly the greatest batsman ever to play in the league. With him is the late Sir Frank Worrell – two of the devastating 'Three W's' who decimated England in the fifties. Weekes played for Bacup.

Sir Donald Bradman, the brightest batting star of all, who changed his mind at the eleventh hour after arranging terms with Accrington in the thirties

Viv Richards, perhaps the most destructive batsman of the last decade, set pulses racing at Rishton in 1987.

E. A. 'Ted' McDonald, the first 'sensation' signing. Later played with Lancashire C.C.C. with great distinction.

Dattu Phadkar, one of the truly great all-rounders – India, Burnley and Nelson.

Amar Singh, India's superb all-rounder, who played for Colne.

A unique picture of South African Jimmy Blanckenberg (centre), Nelson and East Lancashire, who figures in an explosive match of racial hatred when he opposed Constantine in 1929. On his left and right are Harold Hargreaves and Harry Greenwood, photographed after Nelson had won League Championship, Worsley Cup and Junior League Championship in 1928.

Charlie Griffith, West Indies and Burnley . . . did he bowl or throw? His action was never questioned in the league and his bowling record is never likely to be beaten . . . 144 wickets at an average of 5.20 runs each.

Vinoo Mankad, star performer for India against England after being released from his league commitments by Haslingden.

Vijay Hazare, India and Rawtenstall, one of only three to do the league 'double' of 1,000 runs and 100 wickets.

Dennis Lillee, another of the 'greats' in the fast lane, Australia and Haslingden.

Wesley Hall, West Indies speed merchant who played for Accrington.

Johnny Wardle, England, Yorkshire, Rishton and Nelson . . . a complete mixed grill of spin deceits.

Alan Wharton, played for Colne at 13 years of age and turned professional to score no fewer than 17,000 runs for Lancashire, and played once for England.

S. P. 'Fergie' Gupte, the leg spin/googly sorcerer, who played for India and for Rishton.

Roy Gilchrist, West Indies, Bacup and Lowerhouse . . . perhaps the most ferocious and not the least successful of all the league's pacemen.

Neil Hawke, Australia, East Lancashire, Nelson . . . formidable opponent, great companion, tremendously popular professional at both his league clubs.

George Tribe, Australia and Rawtenstall . . . like Wardle could bowl every type of spin in the book.

Bruce Dooland, Australia and East Lancashire . . . another master spinner.

Jack Pettiford, Australia in the 1945 'Victory' Tests, later professional with Kent C.C.C., with Nelson and with Darwen. Popular everywhere.

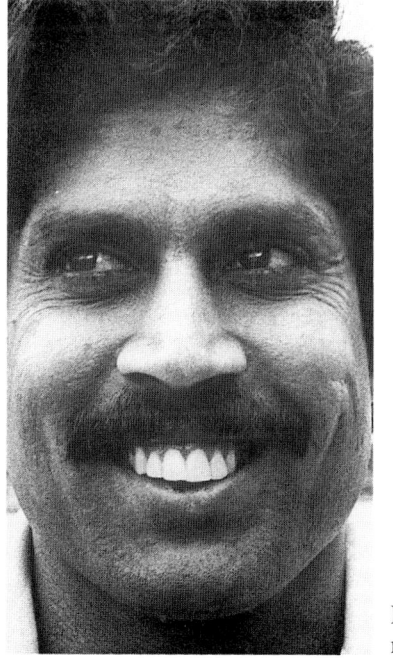

Kapil Dev, one of several Indian all-rounders who have graced the league.

Alan Haigh, wicket-keeper . . . Johnny Wardle said: 'I have never bowled to a better one.' And Wardle had bowled to Godfrey Evans!

Constantine and Pepper, came from India.

Vijay Hazare (Rawtenstall 1949 and 1955), Lala Amarnath (Nelson 1938-39), Vinoo Mankad (Haslingden 1952-53-54-55), Amar Singh (Colne 1935-36-37-38 and Burnley 1939), Dattu Phadkar (Nelson 1951 and Burnley 1960) and Kapil Dev (Nelson 1981) – these were all genuine all-rounders of the highest class.

Hazare, on figures, ranks highest in that he stands alongside Pepper and Colin Miller as one of only three players ever to perform the league's 1,000 runs, 100 wickets 'double' with 1,070 runs and 104 wickets in 1949. He also topped both batting and bowling averages that season.

Mankad, too, on his Test form cannot be ignored by any means.

However, for me, the two who come closest to Constantine and Pepper were Singh and Phadkar.

Hazare was medium pace, swinging the ball with tremendous accuracy. Mankad, of course, was spin, flight and guile.

Amar Singh and Dattu Phadkar, at their peak, were probably the fastest bowlers India has ever produced.

Amar's greatest moment in the league came on the Silver Jubilee Day of King George V and Queen Mary at Seedhill, Nelson, in 1934, the Derby game between the then bitterest of rivals, Nelson and Colne.

There was an all-pay 'gate' of £360 – in what is now $2^1/_2$p a time – under a sun fit for the equator. A crowd of some 12,000!

Colne, batting first, had scored 164, with their highly talented amateur Leslie Bulcock top scorer with 46.

Then Amar Singh, a Goliath of a man, set to work with one of the best bowling displays ever seen in the league.

At that time, of course, Nelson had a side generally considered to be of Minor Counties standard, but only Constantine withstood Amar's tremendous speed attack of guided missiles which reared into the midriff off a perfect length. He scored 51. The rest of the Nelson batsmen could contribute only token scores. When the last pair came to the wicket Nelson required 12 runs to win and Amar, already with eight wickets to his credit, was rampant.

Alf Pollard, the Nelson captain, and Freddie Dowden, the

wicket-keeper, were the tail-end batsmen in this tense situation. Amar and Bulcock were the bowlers.

Dowden swung – and missed! However, Colne's Ellis Dickinson, among the best wicket-keepers the league has ever seen, for once missed the stumping chance of a lifetime. Another unsuccessful appeal for lbw by Amar brought a roar from the crowd. Tension heightened to snapping point as the score difference gradually dwindled – in singles.

Eight runs wanted. Seven. Six. Five. Four. Three. Two.

And then just one run wanted for Nelson to win.

Pollard faced Amar Singh. Was beaten. Pads were rapped. Every Colne voice roared an appeal.

And the umpire's fatal index finger went up.

Amar Singh's contribution to the tie was a wicket haul of 9 for 61.

Constantine told me: 'It was great bowling, really great. Even I had a bruise or two – but, of course, my bruises show up white!'

It was a Worsley Cup match and Nelson went on to win the replay at Colne before another enormous crowd.

Dattu Phadkar was the Indian player who pleased me most. When he first came to the league he was the fastest Indian bowler most of us had ever seen. His out-swinger, pitched off and middle, would veer away into the slips just as the batsman was committed to prod myopically forward. His in-swinger dipped very late. He could also bowl off-spin on a perfect length and occasionally he would throw in a less perfect googly.

As a batsman he could either defend or attack, as needs dictated, with equally flawless technique.

His most majestic shot was surely his square cut. He would lean almost lazily on the back foot and, blade downwards, strike the ball half a yard wide of gully with the crack of a rifle shot. He could also pull devastatingly, and I remember when he took a century off Todmorden's excellent leg-spinner Eric Denison he repeatedly stepped outside his off stump to smash the ball against the spin into the leg-side crowd to such effect that one gnarled old timer who had seen it all before and more was moved to pay the ultimate compliment – 'Connie couldn't a' dun ony better than that,' he said.

Sadly Nelson were not to act too wisely in their dealings with Phadkar later on. In 1951 he was the hero, the first cricketer to all but lay Constantine's ghost. The crowd loved him. When he came back to the club in 1953, however, with a two-season contract to fulfil, it soon became obvious that he was ill with something akin to pneumonia. When he recovered he was still clearly not match fit and Nelson's committee of the day, instead of biding its time, to its discredit tried to break Phadkar's contract on grounds which could not legally be upheld, and on a financial settlement which was ludicrous.

Dattu came to see me at my home the morning after the Nelson committee had shocked him with its decision. I took him to a solicitor – Alec Birtwell, himself a former Nelson and, indeed, Lancashire player, in fact – and it was blatantly evident that the club had no legal grounds at all to back up its appalling misreading of its own contract. The club backed off. It had no option. However, the damage had been done. Relations between the player and the club could never be the same and Nelson Cricket Club lost a player who for many seasons might have done for them in the fifties what Constantine did in the thirties.

Instead Dattu, a lovely man as well as a brilliant cricketer, went to Rochdale in the Central Lancashire League before coming back to Burnley.

At Rochdale he took 152 wickets, which was then a record for that league. At Burnley, nine years after his Nelson debut, he came within a few runs of being the third man to do the double.

I think those figures emphasise what was Nelson Cricket Club's biggest clanger in the club's history, and also elevate Dattu Phadkar to the top half-dozen league all-rounders of all time.

Chapter Six

Tiny Giant of Them All

There have, of course, been hundreds of outstanding amateurs during the league's one hundred years; amateurs in their 'teens, thrown straight from the East Lancashire textile mills, workshops and offices into the maelstrom of cricket at international level, on pitches decidedly below even average county standards.

Twenty-year-olds, nineteen-year-olds, even sixteen-year-olds, with only schoolboy cricket to recommend them, thrust into the front line against the likes of Lindwall and Griffith and Gilchrist and Hall with no first-class experience, few early skills and no helmets to shield them.

The best of them made it. And there were a helluva lot of the best.

There is no way I can deal with them in this chapter without leaving out scores of outstanding cricketers.

I can only, once again, dip into the treasure chest of league lore and memories and nudge a few thoughts in the minds of those who likewise dip into this book.

I think of people like Clifford 'Chick' Hawkwood, who captained and opened innings for Nelson when I first began reporting league cricket in 1947.

Chick was a splendidly 'correct' batsman who, in between his amateur years with the Nelson club, had played several seasons with Lancashire and had, indeed, scored a century at Headingley against probably the best White Rose side ever assembled – the consistently triumphal tykes of the thirties.

I think of Winston Place, of Rawtenstall, who, of course, served Lancashire and England with distinction for many seasons after the war, and of Peter Wood who only last season smashed the Club's and the League's amateur record with a total aggregate of 1,227 runs.

I think of David Lloyd and his son Graham, both graduating from Accrington to Old Trafford and, in David's case, to England level with nine Test matches and a Test double century – 214 against India – to show for it.

I think of Alan Wharton, of Colne, who matured from league amateur to open both batting and bowling for Lancashire in the days of Cyril Washbrook and Brian Statham. Alan is one of Lancashire's all-time top ten when it comes to his aggregate of runs for the county – no fewer than 17,000. And another 5,000 for Leicestershire. He also, of course, played for England.

I think of Les Bulcock, also nurtured on Colne's Horsfield ground, who was offered terms by Glamorgan before becoming one of the finest all-round professionals in the Central Lancashire, Bolton and Bradford leagues.

Still from Colne, Andrew Kennedy and Geoff Hall, opening batsman and opening bowler who both made the grade in county cricket, Les Bulcock's son, Brian, who played for Lancashire II and had trials with Kent, and currently Paul Simmonite.

From Burnley I think of Derek Riley and Bobby Entwistle and Bruce Pairaudeau, Peter Wight and Roland Harrison; many others. Riley, of course, became one of the finest opening batsmen and shrewdest captains ever to play in the league; Entwistle, who modelled himself on Riley, went on to play for Lancashire; Pairaudeau played for the West Indies; and Harrison currently holds the Burnley club's batting aggregate record with 893 runs scored in 1975.

Over at Todmorden, the Lancashire League's only Yorkshire club, several names who graduated from the Centre Vale ground to higher levels of the game come to mind – Derek Shackleton, Hampshire and England; Harold Dawson, Hampshire; Ken Fiddling, Yorkshire and Northants; Dick Horsfall, Essex; Peter Lever, Lancashire and England; Peter Greenwood, Lancashire.

From Accrington, in addition to the Lloyds, the names of Alan Worswick and Eddie Robinson rank high; from Nelson, in addition to Hawkwood, Clarrie Winslow, Johnny Greenwood,

Alec Birtwell, Ian Clarkson, Pat Calderbank and Frank Taylor, the only man to captain two teams (Nelson and Colne) to League and Cup 'double' triumphs; from East Lancashire Ronnie Davies, Frank Hopwood, Tom Dickinson and David Pearson; from Lowerhouse Ernest Smith and Steve Gee; from Haslingden, Les Warburton, Bryan Knowles, George Parker, John Entwistle and Ian Austin.

Haslingden's Warburton, though turning down the chance of cricket professionalism in preference for a banking career, gained unique distinction by becoming the only Lancashire League amateur to figure in an England Test trial; and Austin and Entwistle gained minor immortality – at the Bent Gate ground, at any rate – by establishing a league third-wicket record partnership of 268 runs.

When we come to Bacup we promptly think of Fred Hartley, who from amateur status there became one of the best bowling professionals of the fifties for Church, rivalling even the Australian spin wizards Pepper and Dooland in the bowling averages; and we think also of Vince Broderick, Dick Haworth, John Kelly and the Cooper brothers, who all achieved county status; and, of course, of players like John Usher, Stan Entwistle, Jack Dunham and Peter Bancroft.

At Church there have been the Tommy Lowes, senior and junior, Jack Houldsworth and Sam Pilkington; at Ramsbottom Billy Whitworth and his opening partner John Pearson; at Rishton Jim Smith, Arthur Ramsbottom and Jack Chew; at Enfield Jack Simmons, Jack Riley, Bernard Reidy and Edward Slinger.

One amateur bowler who surely eclipsed all others was, of course, Alf Pollard, the right-arm leg spinner who for many years right up to the 1939-45 war baffled all the league's top batsmen, professional and amateur alike, with his guile, flight and deadly accuracy. Alf played for Colne and then for Nelson, and for both clubs took over one hundred wickets in a season. During his career with the two clubs he took 1,390 wickets, and whilst playing for Nelson against Church in the twenties when there were two completed innings with Nelson finally winning by nine wickets inside four hours, Alf's figures were: 16 overs, 6 maidens,

20 runs, 12 wickets – average runs per wicket, 1.66!

Alf bowled leg spin, as I say, plus a top spinner, but no googly. He was truly a remarkable bowler by any standards.

I realise, as I said at the outset of this chapter, that many outstanding amateurs are omitted from this mere flirtation with the league's history and I offer my apologies to those who will quite justifiably feel they might have been included. My only excuse is that the subject would require more than a chapter – it would demand an encyclopaedia!

One amateur so far not mentioned, however, has deliberately been left until last because he must rank as the tiny giant of them all in the league's Hall of Fame.

I refer, of course, to Enfield's Eddie Paynter.

Eddie was the man who earned Test immortality by leaving his sick bed in Brisbane General Hospital to win The Ashes for England in the most controversial and infamous Test series of all time – the 'Bodyline' tour of Australia in 1933.

This was the Test match, the fourth in the series, where little Eddie defied his doctors and turned up at Brisbane Cricket Ground in pyjamas and dressing gown, and with a raging temperature, ultimately to win the match and the series with a towering last-minute six.

The match itself began on a sour note thanks to the Australians' dislike of Douglas Jardine's 'Bodyline' bowling tactics. 'Bodyline' was in fact an extension of leg-theory bowling. The extension, conceived by Jardine and delivered by Harold Larwood and Bill Voce, was a relentless barrage of fearsome fast bowling from both ends directed with uncommon accuracy at and above the leg stump with a packed leg-side field of forward short leg, two backward short legs, two leg slips, deep fine leg and, of course, wicket-keeper. It was designed to make the batsman defend his body rather than his wicket – and it was tailor made to cut the world's greatest batsman ever, Don Bradman, down to size.

It undoubtedly created an atmosphere foreign to the spirit of the game, but whether Jardine was right or wrong to employ it there was no doubt that little Eddie Paynter, of Oswaldtwistle and Enfield, came out of the series a hero lauded by Australians and

Englishmen alike.

It was on the second day of the Test that he became ill and was removed to Brisbane hospital with tonsilitis and a temperature of 102 degrees.

Sunday was a rest day, but on the Monday, facing an Australian first innings total of 340, England were soon in trouble and Eddie, aided and abetted by Voce, slipped out of the hospital in pyjamas and dressing gown despite warnings from the hospital sister that doing so was dangerous, and went out to bat for England. He scored 83 runs before returning to his hospital bed, and then came back for England's second innings to win The Ashes with a hooked six just before lunch on the fifth day.

He came home to be hailed by England – and by Enfield in the heartland of the Lancashire League – as one of Sport's immortals.

Eddie was presented with the cricket ball which he had hit for six, and a couple of years ago, after his demise, it was sold at Christies for £4,400. We can only hope that whoever bought it treasures it as much as he did.

Chapter Seven

Howzat!

The reader may have noticed that in the previous chapter, apart from a fleeting reference to Ken Fiddling, of Todmorden, there was no mention of wicket-keepers among those amateurs who have graced the league game over the years.

The omission was deliberate in that it seems to me as unequivocal as an Ellis Dickinson 'Howzat!' that this special breed demand a slot of their own.

The Lancashire League has bristled with wicket-keepers of the highest quality.

Dickinson, of Colne, was one; an outstanding 'keeper and a great character.

Born in Earby when that little town was officially in Yorkshire, Ellis played for the White Rose second eleven at a time when that county was able to field what was probably the best club side of all time. It was the era of Sutcliffe, Hutton, Leyland, Mitchell, Barber, Bowes, Verity and, behind the first team stumps, Arthur Wood.

There are some who feel that Ellis would have either deposed or succeeded Wood had he pressed his claims, but instead he joined Colne in the league and stayed to complement some of the best speed and spin world cricket could offer for twenty-two glorious seasons.

Geronimo screaming for a scalp at the head of his Apaches is said to have produced history's most terrifying human sound.

Ellis Dickinson's appeal to the square-leg umpire for a stumping came a close second. They say he once appealed so magnificently on the Horsfield at Colne that an umpire's index finger shot up at Alexandra Meadows in Blackburn! I cannot vouch for the truth of that, but certainly Ellis was possessed of diaphragm and larynx such as no other wicket-keeper of my acquaintance.

There is a lovely tale about him when he was playing against Rawtenstall.

Australia's orthodox left-arm spinner Jack Manning was the bowler as Rawtenstall's No. 9 walked to the crease.

'Listen lad,' said Ellis as the youngster took guard to face his first delivery. 'Listen, ah'll gi' thee some advice. There's nowt for playing back to these Aussie spinners. Tha 'as to go for'ard . . . get to t' ball afore it 'as a chance to spin . . . for'ard, for'ard . . . kill t' spin . . . it's only way.'

'Thank you, Mr Dickinson,' responded No. 9.

Manning bowled. No. 9, playing for'ard as advised, lifted his back foot half a centimetre. And Ellis whipped off the bails with an exultant and successful 'Howzat!' which shattered half a dozen eardrums on the long-on boundary.

The following Saturday Colne played the same opposition away from home. Again No. 9 came to the wicket. This time he took guard, surveyed the field placings, then turned to Ellis and said politely: 'Afore we start, Mr Dickinson, ah'll thank thee to keep thi bloody advice to thi' sell.'

Was he the league's best-ever 'keeper?

It is impossible to say. However, he was certainly in the top strata. Fiddling, of course, played both for Yorkshire and Northants.

And Jack Jordan, of Rawtenstall and later Burnley, played several seasons with Lancashire and at one time was on the fringe for England. In his county days Jack had the distinction of stumping both Ted Dexter and Peter May off Malcolm Hilton's leg-spin, catching Colin Cowdrey off Brian Statham's out-swing, and stumping Tom Graveney down the leg side off Freddie Moore's medium pace.

He was regarded by Cyril Washbrook, among others, as the second best wicket-keeper in the country when in 1956 he was the leading contender to tour South Africa as deputy to Godfrey Evans. He had, in fact, been told that he was the likely choice, but at the end of the day the selectors voted 3-2 for Brian Taylor of Essex.

Jordan had served his time at Rawtenstall where he forced himself into the first team at the age of 16. He mastered the enormous swing of Hazare, and even stood up to the Indian's medium pace when he switched from out-swing to off-cutters. He faced up to the all-out, left-arm leather lightning of Australia's Alan Walker, the right-arm leg breaks and googlies of Bob Madden, and, of course, the left-arm pure spin magic of the brilliant George Tribe.

And then, joining Lancashire, he had the job of keeping wicket to as versatile a crop of bowlers as you could hope to muster – pace, off-spin, leg-spin both right arm and left, googlies, top spin, the lot.

Statham, Hilton, Kenny Grieves, Roy Tattersall and Tommy Greenhough were the bowlers skipper Washbrook was able to call upon.

Other outstanding 'keepers in the league include Doug Payne who had the responsibility of fathoming S. P. 'Fergie' Gupte's prodigious spin for Rishton in the mid-fifties.

Gupte was not the world's most accurate spin sorcerer, but he was surely the biggest spinner of them all. He could turn the ball almost at right angles and was able to drop it outside the off stump and miss leg with his googly, or pitch a foot wide of leg stump and bring his leg-break back to take middle!

If he was a nightmare to batsmen he would be only slightly less so to the wicket-keeper, but Payne handled him well to establish a record season's 'take' of 53 victims – 40 stumped, 13 caught.

Other wicketkeepers who have caught the eye over the years have been Johnny Town and Syd Taylor of Burnley, Tommy Carrick of Todmorden and Bacup, Jack Holding and Ray Kelly of East Lancashire, Bill Heys of Church, Freddie Dowden who handled Constantine's ferocity at one end and Pollard's spin subtleties at the other during Nelson's golden thirties, many others.

Also in the top bracket, without doubt, was Nelson's Alan Haigh.

Haigh had not Dickinson's operatic virtuosity when it came to appealing. He is of quiet temperament by nature and his questions to the umpire were in accord.

He did not demand instant justice like Dickinson; his appeal was more like that of a learned member of the Bar saying respectfully: 'M'lud, I have presented the evidence . . . the man's foot was, as you could hardly fail to observe, two centimetres over the popping crease when I gathered the ball and quietly removed the off bail . . . Could I press you for your verdict?'

For all his quiet approach to the game, however, Alan Haigh was deadly.

He first kept wicket at Seedhill in Jack Pettiford's day when he was only seventeen years old. Then, following National Service in the RAF, he returned to forge a crucial link with bowlers of the class of Dattu Phadkar, Saeed Ahmed, Geoff Noblet, Neil Hawke, Baloo Gupte and Johnny Wardle.

The latter, of course, bowled every kind of left-arm spin in the book – orthodox leg-breaks, 'Chinamen', googlies, top spin and the occasional quickie off the pitch. He was not one to suffer incompetents gladly.

Yet Wardle said of Haigh: 'I have not bowled to a better keeper.' And Wardle, of course, had bowled to Godfrey Evans!

Chapter Eight

"A Nightingale Sang . . . "

I am not at all sure whether this particular Nightingale ever sang at all in the operatic sense, either in Berkeley Square or Nelson Centre or Todmorden, or anywhere else, though I would rate it a good bet, even heavily odds on, that he has risen to high octave in happy, if inharmonious, renderings of *Nellie Dean* in various watering holes within the vicinity of all fourteen Lancashire League clubs.

It is not quite that sort of singing I am talking about, however.

Alwyn Nightingale 'sang' from behind the wicket in full-throated, pungent manner which stamped him without serious rival as the most effective and popular heckler the league has ever known.

Practically all the league clubs have enjoyed their off-field characters, but Alwyn, who supported Nelson Cricket Club both in the incredible Constantine years and later still, was something special.

If there was a crowd of ten thousand at Nelson's Seedhill ground, as in those days there often was, Alwyn Nightingale would have his own little 'crowd' of around five hundred surrounding him behind the bowler's arm.

He had a voice that would reduce Pavarotti's to a whisper.

He had a sharp wit.

And unlike some of today's lager-lout bawlers he rarely, if ever, swore.

It was Alwyn who, when Rishton paraded one of the first mechanised rollers we had ever seen in the thirties, roared from the Blackburn Road end: 'That's nowt. Th' hoss that pulls roller at Nelson 'as a set o' gold teeth'.

It was Alwyn who yelled to Tommy Lowe senior at Church when Constantine was administering a fearful hiding: 'Tha' as 'im i' two minds, Tommy – he doesn't knaw whether to hit thi for fours or sixes.'

It was Alwyn who, when hauled before Nelson Corporation because of the untidy state of his council house garden, told the City fathers; 'Tell you wot – I'm a sporting chap – you flag it and I'll swill it.'

Alwyn has now passed on to whatever Elysian Spion Kop barrackers pass on to, but in his day he was compulsive listening anywhere.

I remember him umpiring one particular match in which I played at Holt House, Colne; some sort of mills and workshops' encounter. The light was beginning to fade – likewise Alwyn's hopes of getting a pint at the nearby North Valley pub before what was then ten o'clock closing time.

With the last man in and the clock ticking away I bowled. I do not know to this day how or why – it was certainly not due to anything I did – but what was a quite innocuous delivery well outside the off-stump reared off some sort of divot and struck the batsman on the chest.

'Are ta going to appeal?' enquired Alwyn.

'Well, I wasn't thinking of so doing,' I replied.

'No matter,' said Alwyn, 'he's out just t' same.'

Up went the old index finger and Alwyn was ordering his pint in the North Valley before the unfortunate batsman had got his pads off.

Even Constantine had to take a bit of verbal stick off Alwyn if he was not up to scratch, but the two became great friends and I recall one Sunday morning when the West Indian, at that time Trinidad's Minister of Transport, was speaking at Nelson Weavers' Institute, now, of course, Silverman Hall.

Alwyn, Learie and myself adjourned to the nearby Nelson Preparatory Workers' Club – The Dressers, as it is better known – just across the road afterwards.

'Nah then, Connie,' enquired Alwyn – it was always by the affectionate 'Connie' that Learie was known to his Nelson fans –

'Nah then, Connie, wots thi' poison?'

Learie did not drink all that much in those days and replied: 'Lemonade, please.'

'Lemonade!' snorted Alwyn. 'Lemonade! Look 'ere, tha may be t' Minister o' Transport ower there, but I'm Minister o' Thirst 'ere and if we 'ave to drink this stuff they call mild ale 'ere then it'll 'ave to be good enough for thee. Tha'll 'ave a pint of mild.'

'Reight lad,' said Learie, 'a pint it'll be.'

We talked cricket and, as always when Learie was around, a crowd gathered and laughter reigned.

'Where are you working now, Alwyn?' Learie asked.

'In Bradford,' returned Alwyn. 'Mucky 'ole; never seen a place muckier – even t' mice wear boiler suits.'

There have, of course, been many other characters over the years, both on and off the field of play.

Edwin Cragg, the groundsman at Lowerhouse before the war, was one. He would be up at five o'clock in the morning chimney sweeping and then move straight to Lowerhouse's West End ground to carry out his groundsman's chores.

One day East Lancashire were the visitors and the pitch was wet.

Ronnie Davies was the Blackburn club's skipper – an excellent batsman, a kind man, but with a touch of the autocratic old school.

'Sawdust, groundsman!' Davies ordered.

'Reight,' answered Edwin from inside the groundsman's hut, dallying a moment to gulp down his last drop of ale.

Davies was impatient. 'Sawdust, groundsman!' he repeated, and this time it was more an ultimatum than a request.

'Reight, reight, ahm coming as fast as ah can,' shouted Edwin. 'Wot sort dosta want – oak or mahogany?'

On the field, of course, Cec Pepper was the banterer supreme.

It was Pepper who, when asked by his Burnley skipper Derek Riley where he would like his fieldsmen placed, rapped: 'Oh, just led the sods wander about as they please – I can bowl this bloody lot out.'

It was Pepper who after bowling a baffling mixture of spin at Colne, but missing both bat and stumps, shouted down the wicket to the bemused batsman: 'Right, you can open your bloody eyes now – I've finished.'

It was Pepper who was once no-balled at Bacup twice in two deliveries. He glared at the umpire, but said nothing, just marked out a new run-up and cleaned the ball in the sawdust behind the wicket. In he wheeled to bowl again, but this time he deliberately over-stepped the bowling mark and the umpire's cry was inevitable – 'No ball!'

'Too bloody right, mate,' snapped Pepper, whipping round to show the umpire an empty right hand, 'the bloody ball is back there in the sawdust!'

Pepper was once bowling to India's Gul Mohammad, then Ramsbottom's professional. The Indian had nicked his leg-breaks and googlies repeatedly without managing to get himself out, and Pepper asked him at the end of one over: 'What do you do with your old bats?'

'What do you mean?' asked Mohammad.

'Put it this way,' retorted Pepper, 'let me have 'em in future – middles must be brand new.'

Another outstanding character on the field was, of course, Alec Birtwell, who has probably the unique distinction of playing for four different Lancashire League clubs – Nelson, Colne, Burnley and Lowerhouse – through residential and business qualifications.

Alec, a solicitor, was an amateur who bowled googlies – albeit somewhat transparent googlies – before most and, indeed, bowled them for Lancashire County.

At cricket, at table tennis, in court as a solicitor, at social functions, Alec was a wit with a dogged approach to any situation which infuriated players and spectators alike.

The odd thing was that he actually liked being barracked. And the bigger the crowd the more he liked it.

Once, while playing for Lancashire against Kent in 1937, he rated all the facile majesty of Neville Cardus, no less, in what was then the *Manchester Guardian*.

In league cricket Alec always batted at 9, 10 or 11 – 'down at Faith, Hope and Charity,' as he himself described it. The Lancashire captain of the day, however, sent him in as nightwatchman and Alec was still there at lunch the following day, delighting in stonewalling everything the Kent bowlers, including England's Douglas Wright, could throw at him with a dead-pan face and an even more dead-pan bat for a mere thirty runs.

Cardus wrote, under the headline 'Eerie innings by Birtwell,' and referred to him as 'a more or less agile sandbag.'

'Birtwell,' said Cardus, 'held all the known laws of cause and effect in suspension and somehow batted in a void beyond the reach of mortal bowler.'

'I regret to say,' Cardus ended his column, 'that after lunch Birtwell attempted strokes. A number of pedants in the crowd sarcastically cheered his masterly strokelessness and catchlessness. Birtwell struck an irrelevant two and then, endeavouring to repeat the stroke, he sliced to Woolley, who held the catch one-handed. Thus ambition was Birtwell's down fall, as it was Napoleon's.'

Many people would have been more than upset at Cardus's piece and, indeed, Alec's father, also a solicitor, talked about sueing.

Alec, himself, however, loved it.

He gave a bit of stick. And he could take a bit of stick. He was a great joker – and like Alwyn Nightingale, Edwin Cragg and Cec Pepper typical of the Lancashire League at its best.

Chapter Nine

Simply, The Best

When it comes to selecting a Lancashire League team to beat the world I have to confine myself, I think, to the period with which I am best acquainted, the post-war years, and I would appoint the captain of that team without hesitation – Australia's Bobby Simpson.

Simpson, who played for Accrington in 1959, stands second only to Weekes in 'time limit' as the league's most prolific batsman on one season's aggregate with 1,444 runs, but he was, of course, an outstanding captain for his country and one of the best slip fielders in the history of the game.

Who do you think he would want as his opening bowler?

I would be surprised if he did not toss the new ball to his fellow Australian Ray Lindwall and say: 'Here you are, Ray . . . give it all you've got.' And, as I have said in an earlier chapter of this book, Lindwall certainly had plenty to give.

Who, then, would be his new-ball partner? Griffith? Tyson? Chester Watson? Dennis Lillee?

Or Michael Holding? It is a great temptation to go for Holding, the West Indian and former Rishton professional. He was very much in the Lindwall mould with a Rolls-Royce run-up and an accuracy beyond reproach. However, in the belief that opposites complement each other in fast bowling partnerships, like Trueman and Statham or Lindwall and Miller, I think I would have to go for Roy Gilchrist. He was probably the fastest and certainly the most ferocious of the post-war speed merchants.

The spinners? Once again the choice is mind boggling. As with the batsmen the list is endless. And, of course, there are several

World Team alternatives to the one which I have chosen. However, for what it is worth here it is in batting order . . .

Bobby Simpson (Australia and Accrington), skipper and opening batsman.

Vijay Hazare (India and Rawtenstall).

Clyde Walcott (West Indies and Enfield).

Everton Weekes (West Indies and Bacup).

Viv Richards (West Indies and Rishton).

Bill Alley (Australia and Colne).

Collie Smith (West Indies and Burnley).

Cec Pepper (Australia and Burnley).

Ray Lindwall (Australia and Nelson).

George Tribe (Australia and Rawtenstall).

Roy Gilchrist (West Indies, Bacup and Lowerhouse).

It is a team with two world-class opening batsmen and packed with safe and explosive batting right down to No. 9, top-class pace bowling, mixed spin both right and left arm, and brilliance in the field.

For wicket-keeper you could choose between Walcott and Alley – they had both 'kept' at top level before coming into the league.

It would take some beating, but there are so many magnificent cricketers omitted – Griffith, Tyson, Phadkar, Wardle, Lock, the Chappell brothers, Alan Border, Conrad Hunte, to name but a few – that I have no doubt the reader will be able to choose an alternative league team to make it The Test of all time.

How many players in the history of the league have taken all ten wickets in an innings?

The answers is – only 21.

And the best analysis is constantine's ten wickets for ten runs against Accrington in 1934. Accrington were all out for twelve runs.

The others to achieve the all-ten feat, all professionals, are Tom Lancaster of Enfield (twice), Cec Pepper of Burnley (twice), Roy Gilchrist of Bacup and Lowerhouse (twice), Fred Hartley of Church (twice), Archie Slater of Bacup (twice), A. W. Hallam

(Nelson), A. Kermode (Bacup), Billy Cook (Burnley), H. Harrison (Haslingden), J. Horsley (Nelson), E. Achong (Burnley), H. Robson (Haslingden), Fred Freer (Rishton), S. P. Gupte (Rishton), Wes Hall (Accrington), A. Ferraira (Nelson), Ted McDonald (Nelson), F. Slater (Enfield), A. J. Richardson (Burnley), and A. E. Nutter (Nelson).

I have deliberately tried not to clutter up this tribute to the world's greatest cricket league by introducing too many statistics. A few, however, are so remarkable that they border on the miraculous, and I am grateful to that excellent annual publication, the *Lancashire Cricket League Official Handbook,* which I strongly recommend devotees of the league game to purchase, for much of the following information.

Two players, for instance, have performed double hat-tricks during the league's long history.

One was Joe Boon, who performed the feat for Burnley against Rawtenstall in 1930 – all clean bowled.

The other was Fergie Gupte with a haul of eight wickets for 19 runs for Rishton against Accrington on Whit Tuesday 1956.

There are a good many nine-wicket bowling performances, but the most notable was surely that of Australian Fred Freer when playing for Rishton against Enfield on 15th May 1948, he took – nine wickets for just three runs!

I remember that Alec Birtwell, who I have mentioned in an earlier chapter, was defending solicitor in a court case at Nelson the following Saturday morning. Nelson were to play Rishton that same afternoon and at that time BBC Radio was running a gripping and highly popular thriller series called 'Appointment With Fear.'

Alec addressed the magistrates thus; 'I wonder, Your Worships, if I could persuade you to take my case first since I have a traumatic day ahead of me . . . this afternoon I have an Appointment With Freer!'

Leslie Bulcock, of Colne, is one of the few amateurs who have performed the nine-wicket feat. He was only 19 years old when he took 9 for 31 against Rishton in 1932.

A. Bourke is another – 9 for 35 for Church against Rawtenstall in 1961.

M. Hartley took 9 for 13 for Todmorden against Bacup, including a hat-trick, in 1976 – and that was after conceding ten runs in his first over!

R. Taylor took 9 for 42 – seven clean bowled – for Haslingden against Colne in 1982.

Nick Westwell took 9 for 83 for Church against lowerhouse in 1985.

Jack Houldsworth of Church and Pat Calderbank of Nelson are two amateurs who have taken over 1,000 league wickets during their respective careers in the league.

Another, of course, is the great Alf Pollard, who in 19 seasons with Nelson and Colne, amassed a total of 1,390 wickets.

Alan Worswick and Eddie Robinson, of Accrington, created a league record by taking 158 wickets between them in 1970 – no other two amateurs ever having taken so many wickets for one club in any one season.

Only two seasons ago Craig Smith of Rishton joined the highly exclusive band of amateurs to have scored over 1,000 runs in a season; others being Bryan Knowles and George Parker of Haslingden, and Joe Midgley of Bacup back in 1929.

Knowles, indeed, has established himself as one of the most outstanding amateur batsmen in the league's history, and has played and captained League Cricket Conference elevens against tourists from the West Indies, India, Sri Lanka and Australia.

In the summer of 1982 Collis King, the West Indian professional for Colne, scored 42 runs in one over which included two no balls – 4, 6, 4, 4, 6, 6, 4, 2, 6, 0.

There are, of course, numerous other batting and bowling feats which have given Lancashire league cricket an incomparable sparkle over the years since this closely-knit circle of Lancashire mill towns, as they once were, banded together to bring many of the world's greatest performers to the Red Rose hills and valleys to give the league a status renowned and second to none wherever the game of cricket is played.

I hope, with this book, I have helped readers to share some of the most glorious moments which have decorated the league's history.

Chapter Ten

One Hundred Years On

I have to close this admittedly long look back to yesterday's Lancashire League glories with a deserved reference to the present.

In doing that I have to refer unstintingly to Peter Sleep's magnificent batting performance whilst with Rishton last summer.

Sleep, a South Australian in his mid-thirties, has now moved on to league pastures elsewhere, but as a batsman of quality and a right-arm leg-spin bowler has won many friends in the Lancashire League, first at East Lancashire, and in the 1990-91 seasons at Rishton. He has played in fifteen Tests – against England, Pakistan, India and New Zealand, and as a spin bowler able to turn the ball quite considerably both ways he is inscrutable, uncommon in this age of all-out speed.

It has been as a batsman, however, that he has inscribed his name in the record books when last season, with a massive aggregate of 1,621 runs in 26 innings, he shattered Everton Weekes' record of 1,518 which had stood for forty years.

It has to be taken into account, of course, that the rules governing the league game have changed vastly since the Weekes' days: the boundaries are shorter, the six hits much, much easier. And Peter Sleep's 1991 average of 81.05 against Weeks 158.25 in the fifties, does not alter my previous acclaim for the West Indian as the greatest batsman the league has ever seen. Even so Sleep's performance last season clearly ranks very highly in the Centenary year roll of honours.

Sleep, an affable companion in any pavilion bar, is deadly

serious whenever he takes to the field, either in a match or in coaching sessions. He told me: 'There is no point in turning up for practice if you are not going to take it seriously. Whatever faults a team might have on the field you have to try to iron them out off it. That's the way to win – and I want to win. The time to relax is after the game.'

Another of the present crop of league professionals who have in recent years seriously rivalled – though I cannot honestly say say surpassed – the golden oldies is another South Australian, Colin Miller, who in recent seasons has performed exceptionally well for Rawtenstall.

Miller, as mentioned in an earlier chapter, joined fellow Australian Cec Pepper and Indian Vijay Hazare in a rare trio who have accomplished the league 'double' by scoring 1,000 runs and taking 100 wickets.

Pepper and Hazare achieved their feats as far back as 1949; Miller joined them in 1990, taking 100 wickets (plus another 23 in the Worsley Cup competition) and scoring 1,078 runs.

Last season he again took over 100 wickets to finish second in the bowling averages and scored 780 runs.

There have been other exciting professionals in recent years – Roger Harper at Bacup, Geoff Lawson, the Australian Test fast bowler, and Simon O'Donnell at Haslingden, Paul Reiffel at East Lancashire, Joe Scuderi at Nelson.

O'Donnell, of course, fought his way back to play Lancashire League cricket and then to win back his Australian Test place after beating cancer.

Five years ago he was celebrating Australia's World Cup victory over England in Calcutta and forty-eight hours later, back in Australia, he went for what he thought was a routine check on a slight swelling and was told: 'It's cancer.'

'I was devastated,' he told me at Haslingden one day in 1989. 'Slowly it dawned on me that I had to get down to business. I had to fight this thing. I had to go out and win.'

There was chemotherapy treatment and also operations which removed two of Simon's ribs and a couple of glands.

And that summer, two years after the disease was diagnosed, O'Donnell was spearheading the Haslingden club to its third championship in three seasons. Since, of course, he has reclaimed his Test place on the Australian scene.

The young Scuderi is yet another Australian who, last season, proved himself to be an outstanding crowd-pleaser for Nelson. Some of his innings were electric – some even said rivalling Constantine's! Though it has to be added that those who said it had probably never seen Constantine. Even so Scuderi established himself as undoubtedly one of the most popular and effective professionals Nelson, with all their Test-class, big-name signings of the past, have ever had.

He scored 1,414 runs at an average of 67 and took 75 wickets at 19's. It will be good to see him back with the Seedhill club this summer.

All in all the one hundredth birthday of the Lancashire League sees most of the clubs, now modernised and miles removed from the mill chimney background of their embryo days of 1892, in optimistic, forward-looking frame of mind.

The future promises many more days of glorious cricket in the sun.

Days of outstanding deeds with bat and ball, of banter in the pavilions, of characters and cricket lore in the hostelries of this small corner of Lancashire which has gained world-wide fame through international cricketers from all points of the compass.

The League may never again quite deify the Constantines as it did in the days before television familiarised us with the world's most glittering stars.

However, it will survive. It will thrive. It will continue to brighten our lives.

For another one hundred years?

That will be for somebody else's pen to record!

Noel Wild has been an outstanding journalist in Lancashire for over fifty years.

He was editor of the *Nelson Leader*, the *Colne Times* and the *Barnoldswick and Earby Times* for more than a quarter of a century, and both before and since his retirement from full-time work in 1987 he has established himself as a freelance writer for both the national and provincial press.

His weekly column 'On The Wild Side' for the *Lancashire Evening Telegraph* for the past four years has been widely read.

Though he has written on a variety of topics over the years, sport in general and cricket in particular – Lancashire League cricket specifically – always predominated.

He has enjoyed close personal friendships with many of the league's best-known cricketers, professionals and amateurs alike, and, indeed, much of this book, with its observations and intimate discussions with players like the great Learie Constantine, could only have been written by someone who knows the game, and the men who played it during the League's most glorious decades, so well.